the perfect guide for new cooks

beginners
STEP-BY-STEP

beginners
STEP-BY-STEP

the perfect guide for new cooks

This edition published in 2012
LOVE FOOD is an imprint of Parragon Books Ltd

Parragon
Queen Street House
4 Queen Street
Bath BA1 1HE, UK

ISBN: 978-1-4454-8282-8

Printed in China

Photography by Mike Cooper
Home economy by Lincoln Jefferson
Cover design by Geoff Borin
Internal design by Talking Design
Introduction by Linda Doeser
New recipes by Christine France
Edited by Fiona Biggs

Notes for the Reader
This book uses standard kitchen measuring spoons and cups. All spoon and cup measurements are level unless otherwise indicated. Unless otherwise stated, milk is assumed to be whole, eggs are large, individual vegetables are medium, and pepper is freshly ground black pepper. Unless otherwise stated, all root vegetables should be washed and peeled before using. Scrub all fruits and vegetables with plain water to remove any pesticides, dirty or bacterial contamination. Remove and discard the outer leaves of leafy greens.

For best results, use a food thermometer when cooking meat and poultry; check the latest USDA guidelines for current advice.

Garnishes and serving suggestions are all optional and not necessarily included in the recipe ingredients or method. The times given are only an approximate guide. Preparation times differ according to the techniques used by different people and the cooking times may also vary from those given. Optional ingredients, variations, or serving suggestions have not been included in the calculations.

Recipes using raw or very lightly cooked eggs should be avoided by infants, the elderly, pregnant women, and people with weakened immune systems. Pregnant and breast-feeding women are advised to avoid eating peanuts and peanut products. People with nut allergies should be aware that some of the prepared ingredients used in the recipes in this book may contain nuts. Always check the packaging before use.

contents

introduction

This wonderful cookbook, with its profusion of superlative and truly helpful photographs, will prove to be an invaluable guide and source of reference for those who are new to cooking and those who still approach it with trepidation. The recipes are clear, easy to follow, beautifully illustrated, and simply delicious, so whether you've never even boiled an egg or you want to build on a little experience, you are certain of success every time.

Each recipe starts with a photograph of all its ingredients, but this is far more than just a colorful picture—or even less helpful—a montage that is not to scale, so that a mushroom looks the same size as an egg. Instead, it serves as an at-a-glance way of checking that you have everything ready before you start cooking. Just comparing the picture with the ingredients arranged on your own counter or kitchen table will help make sure that you don't forget something, and when it's time to add the onion, for example, you have already diced it as specified in the ingredients list. If you are uncertain about how coarsely to shred cheese or how thinly to slice carrots, a glance at the photograph will provide an instant answer.

Each short and easy-to-follow step of the method is explained without any jargon or incomprehensible technical terms. Once again, what you see in the photograph is what you should expect to see in front of you. This is reassuring and will boost your confidence when, for example, you're not certain how browned the chops should be before starting the next step. Finally, every recipe ends with a mouthwatering photograph of the finished dish.

Why you need this book

Learning to cook can seem like a daunting task, and television chefs who chop vegetables at an unfeasible speed while simultaneously making a sauce and a salad and talking to a camera only serve to make the prospect seem even more terrifying. However, once you start, you'll be surprised to discover just how easy

and enjoyable it is to rustle up tasty and nourishing snacks, dinners, desserts, and sweet treats.

In this book, there are 60 fuss-free recipes for all occasions and every taste from pasta to pot roast and from muffins to cheesecake. In no time at all, you will master techniques from carving a chicken to frosting a cake and have a substantial basic kitchen repertoire at your fingertips. From Get Started through Novice and Intermediate to Advanced, using this book is like having an experienced chef in your kitchen to guide you.

tips for beginners

> Read all the way through the recipe—ingredients list and method—before you start, so that you know exactly what you will need. Scrabbling about at the back of a cupboard to find the right spice or rummaging in a drawer for a wooden spoon in the middle of cooking a dish is, at best, irritating and, at worst, liable to result in a burned offering instead of a delicious meal.

> Collect all your ingredients together and make sure that they are ready to use— for example, visible fat trimmed from meat and vegetables peeled. In addition, do any initial preparation described in the ingredients list, such as shredding cheese. Check the photograph.

> Arrange the plates and bowls of ingredients in the order in which they are to be used. That way, you will be unlikely to overlook something. If a number of ingredients, such as flavorings and spices, will be added at the same time, put them in small piles or in egg cups on the same plate.

> Don't be tempted to skip any stages in the method—they are there for a reason. If the recipe requires milk to be heated before it is added to other ingredients, for example, don't just grab a carton straight from the refrigerator because you may end up with a lumpy sauce.

> Allow for plenty of time. If you try to rush, you will be more likely to make a mistake or hurt yourself on a hot dish or with a sharp knife.

> Don't be overambitious when deciding on a menu. A cold appetizer or soup prepared in advance, ready for reheating, and fresh fruit for dessert will give you time to focus on preparing the main dish. When you've had some practice and gained confidence, you can be more adventurous.

> When adding seasonings, especially hot spices, but also salt and pepper, err on the side of caution. Add a little, then taste and, if necessary, add a little more.

> When you have finished with utensils, move them out of your way. A work area cluttered with sticky spoons, a used cutting board, and a gooey mixing bowl is not an efficient space.

> Be careful when cooking with oil and never leave the pan unattended. Do not fill a deep-fryer more than one-third full. If you are unavoidably called away, turn off the heat. More than half of house fires start in the kitchen. Also turn saucepans so that the

handles don't stick out over another burner or the edge of the stove, and remember to turn the oven off when you have finished.

time-saving shortcuts

> Ovens and broilers take time to heat up, so if you're going to be using either of them, turn them on to preheat when you first go into the kitchen.

> Some ingredients, such as ham, bacon, smoked salmon, anchovy fillets, dried fruit, pitted olives, and many fresh herbs, can be snipped into pieces with scissors more quickly and easily than chopping with a knife. Green beans and snow peas can also be trimmed with scissors.

> Tearing lettuce and delicate herbs, such as basil, with your fingers is quicker than chopping them.

> To peel garlic, lightly crush a clove with the flat blade of a chef's knife. This makes the skin easy to remove.

> When chopping chocolate, first dip the knife blade into hot water and dry it. Dipping a measuring spoon into hot water, then drying it, makes it easier to measure small quantities of sticky ingredients, such as honey and syrup. Speed up cake making by rinsing the bowl with boiling water, then drying before beating together the butter and sugar.

> When boiling root vegetables, such as carrots, make a shallow layer in a large saucepan instead of a deep layer in a smaller pan so that they cook more quickly and evenly.

> If the recipe calls for softened butter and you have forgotten to remove it from the refrigerator, microwave it on High for 15–20 seconds.

> The smaller ingredients are, the faster they will cook. Finely dicing and chopping vegetables will speed up the cooking time and, if you use a food processor to do this, you will speed up the preparation time.

> You can marinate meat in advance, then freeze it until the day you want to cook it.

> Remember that you don't have to make everything from scratch with fresh ingredients. Take advantage of really useful convenience ingredients, some of which have extra benefits in addition to being time-saving. Canned tomatoes, for example, have far more flavor than fresh ones that have to be picked before they ripen. Other useful canned goods include corn kernels and beans, such as chickpeas. Ready-to-bake rolled dough pie crust and prepared vegetables also speed up food preparation without loss of quality.

> Don't throw the ends of loaves of bread away. Tear them up and process in a blender or food processor

11

>1 >2 >3

to make breadcrumbs, then store them in the freezer until required for a recipe. This is economical. too. You can also grate lemon and lime rinds after squeezing the fruits for their juice and store the grated rind in plastic food bags in the freezer.

useful equipment

As a general rule, it is worth buying the best-quality kitchen equipment you can afford because it will be more efficient and last longer.

> **Measuring cups:** Dry ingredients are often measured by volume, using a set of standard kitchen measuring cups that come in ¼ cup, ⅓ cup, ½ cup, and 1 cup sizes. Bring the blunt edge of the blade of a knife across the rim of the cup to level the ingredients and, if measuring brown sugar, first pack it into the cup before leveling it.

> **Measuring spoons:** When recipes specify spoons, they mean standard kitchen measuring spoons, not ordinary tablespoons and teaspoons. Sets consist of 1 tablespoon, 1 teaspoon, ½ teaspoon, and ¼ teaspoon. To measure dry ingredients, as with measuring cups, level with a knife blade.

> **Liquid measuring cup:** You'll find markings along the side of the cup to indicate the measurements by volume. Look at the lines at eye level for accurate reading. These measuring cups are available in a variety of sizes, shapes, and materials. A heatproof cup is useful, and a tall, thin, translucent cup is easier to use than a short, fat, opaque one.

> **Saucepans:** Start with three or four pans in different sizes that have heavy bottoms, tight-fitting lids, and heatproof handles on both pans and lids. You can add to them as you become more proficient and assured about the style of cooking that suits you. Avoid sets of pans because they often include at least one pan that you never use. Nonstick linings are a matter of personal choice.

> **Skillets:** A 9–11-inch heavy skillet with sloping sides has a multitude of uses from cooking eggs to searing fish. Nonstick pans mean that you use less fat and are easier to clean, but because sediment doesn't stick to the bottom of the pan, they cannot be deglazed for making sauces and gravies. A smaller pan is useful for omelets, pancakes, and toasting seeds, nuts, and spices.

> **Knives:** Heavy, well-balanced knives are essential in any kitchen. Start with a chef's, utility, paring, and vegetable knife and add to them as you go along. A carving knife is also necessary if you plan to cook roasts. Store them in a knife block to prevent the edge of the blades from being chipped, and sharpen the knives frequently. Blunt knives are not only inefficient but can also slip more easily.

>4 >5 >6

>1 >2 >3

14

> **Cutting boards:** It is important to have a few for separate use, with at least one each for raw meat, poultry, and fish, and another one for vegetables and fruit to avoid cross-contamination. Plastic boards are available in a range of colors, making it easy to know which one should be used for which ingredients, and they can be sterilized. Many people prefer wood, which, although it can't be sterilized, is naturally antibacterial.

> **Bowls:** You will need various sizes for mixing ingredients and for holding measured ingredients. Bowls may be stainless steel, ceramic, copper, melamine, plain glass, and heatproof, ovenproof, and microwave-proof glass. Some come with a plastic lid, making them useful for storage, too.

> **Strainers:** Wire strainers in various sizes are useful for straining vegetables and sifting dry ingredients (or use a sifter). Because metal can taint the flavor of acid mixtures, have at least one nylon strainer.

> **Spoons, spatulas, and ladles:** Wooden spoons are strong, don't bend, and don't get hot, so they are invaluable for many purposes. It is worth buying a selection of them, some with shaped edges. Spatulas, made from wood, rubber, or plastic are also multipurpose and are especially useful if you have nonstick pans. A large slotted spoon helps to drain ingredients as you lift them out of the pan. A ladle with a good size bowl is perfect for

transferring liquid or semi-liquid ingredients. Make sure it has a pouring lip or a continuous rolled lip to make it easy to pour without spillage and drips.

> **A handheld balloon whisk and mixer:** These can be used for a lot of tasks, such as beating eggs and whisking sauces. A handheld electric mixer will make such tasks even quicker and easier.

> **Oven-to-tableware:** These dual- or even treble-purpose dishes are not necessarily cheap but are good value for money and save time—not so much with cooking, although they can do, but certainly with cleaning up afterward. They may be plain or patterned glass or ceramic and include a vast range of different dishes from casserole dishes to ramekins. Enamel coated, cast-iron dutch ovens distribute heat evenly and look smart, but they are heavy, especially when full, and usually not suitable for the dishwasher.

> **Bakeware:** As there is such an extensive range, it is probably sensible to buy cake pans, muffin pans, loaf pans, tart pans, and so on, as and when you need them. Heavy gauge pans distribute heat evenly and prevent scorching. They are available with nonstick linings. Baking sheets are used for many purposes in addition to making cookies and pastries; buy heavy sheets that won't buckle in the oven or wobble when you lift them out.

get started

easy eggs

serves 4

ingredients

boiled
4 eggs, at room
  temperature

scrambled
8 eggs
¼ cup light cream
  or whole milk
2 tablespoons salted butter
salt and pepper

fried
peanut oil or sunflower oil
4 fresh eggs

poached
4 fresh eggs

Boiled

>1 Place the eggs in a small saucepan and add enough cold water to just cover. Place over high heat until just boiling.

>2 Reduce the heat to a simmer and cook the eggs for 3 minutes for a soft-boiled egg with a runny yolk.

Scrambled

>1 Beat the eggs in a bowl with a fork. Add the cream, season with salt and pepper, and beat again.

>2 Melt the butter in a small, nonstick skillet and stir in the eggs. Stir over medium heat for 1–2 minutes, until almost set, then remove from the heat.

>1 Fried

Heat the oil in a heavy skillet until hot. Carefully break the eggs into the skillet and let set for 30 seconds.

>2

For sunny-side-up eggs, cook for an additional minute, occasionally tilting the skillet and basting the hot oil over the eggs to lightly cook the top surface. Alternatively, for easy-over eggs, flip the eggs over with a spatula and cook for an additional minute.

>1 Poached

Bring 1¼ inches of water to a gentle simmer in a deep saucepan. Carefully break in the eggs.

>2

Let the eggs cook over low heat for 3½–4 minutes, until just set with a runny yolk. Remove with a slotted spoon.

quick omelet

serves 1

ingredients

tomato & bell pepper

2 extra-large eggs
1 teaspoon butter
1 teaspoon sunflower oil
1 small green bell pepper,
 seeded and diced
1 tablespoon olive oil
1 tomato, diced
salt and pepper

mushroom & herbs

2 extra-large eggs
1 tablespoon chopped
 chives
1 tablespoon chopped
 parsley
1 teaspoon sunflower oil
1½ cups thinly sliced white
 button mushrooms
1 teaspoon butter,
 plus extra for frying
salt and pepper

ham & cheese

2 extra-large eggs
1 teaspoon butter
1 teaspoon sunflower oil
⅓ cup chopped, cooked
 sliced ham
½ cup shredded Swiss
 cheese, American cheese,
 or cheddar cheese
salt and pepper

> **1** To start the omelet, break the eggs into a bowl, season with salt and pepper, and lightly beat with a fork. If you are making the Mushroom & Herbs omelet, add the chopped herbs to the eggs.

> **2** Heat a small omelet pan or skillet until hot and add the butter and oil, swirling to coat evenly. Pour in the egg mixture, tilting to spread, and cook for 5 seconds.

> **3** Use a spatula to draw in the edges of the omelet toward the center. Continue until most of the liquid is set.

> **4** **Tomato & bell pepper**
Sauté the chopped bell pepper in the olive oil in a separate skillet, stirring, for 3–4 minutes, until soft. Sprinkle the chopped bell pepper and tomato over one-half of the omelet and fold over the other half.

>5 Mushroom & herbs

Sauté the mushrooms in butter in a separate skillet for 3–4 minutes, sprinkle them over one-half of the omelet, and fold over the other half.

>6 Ham & cheese

Sprinkle the omelet with the ham and half the cheese. Fold over one side to enclose the filling and sprinkle with the remaining cheese.

Serve immediately.

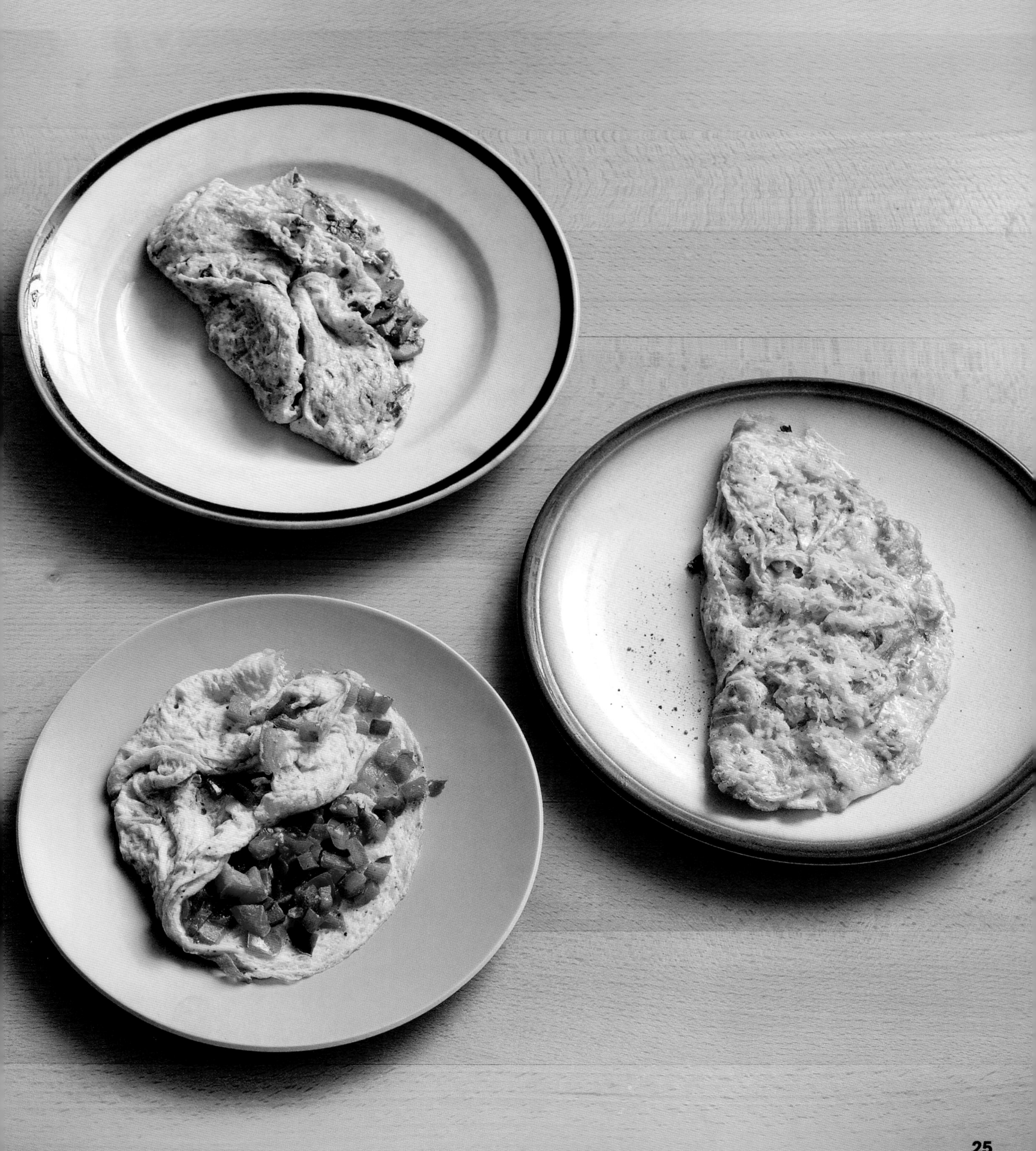

grilled ham & cheese sandwich

makes 1 sandwich

ingredients
2 slices white Italian bread,
  rye bread, or white
  sandwich bread
1½ teaspoons salted butter,
  softened
½ cup shredded Swiss
  cheese
1 slice cooked ham,
  trimmed to fit the bread,
  if necessary

> **>1** Thinly spread each slice of bread on one side with butter, then put one slice on the work surface, buttered side down.

> **>2** Sprinkle half the cheese over the bread up to the edges. Add the ham and the remaining cheese, add the other slice of bread, buttered side up, and press down.

Cut the sandwich in half diagonally and serve immediately.

> **3** Heat a heavy skillet over medium–high heat. Reduce the heat to medium, add the sandwich, and cook on one side for 2–3 minutes, until golden brown.

> **4** Flip the sandwich over with a spatula and cook on the other side for 2–3 minutes, until all the cheese is melted and the bread is golden brown.

perfect steak

serves 4

ingredients

4 tenderloin steaks,
  about 8 ounces each

oil, for brushing
salt and pepper

>1 Heat a heavy skillet over a high heat, until smoking hot. As a general rule, do not cook more than two steaks at a time and keep them spaced well apart. If you add more than two steaks to the pan the temperature will drop too low to sucessfully fry the steaks.

>2 To prevent the steaks from curling up, cut the fatty edge at ½-inch intervals with a sharp knife. Lightly brush with a little olive oil and season with salt and pepper. Steaks can safely be eaten rare or blue, but note that cooking times will vary depending on the type and thickness of the steak, and how hot your skillet is.

>3 For blue, place the steak in a very hot skillet and cook for 1 minute on each side to sear the outside but leave the center very rare. Let stand for 3 minutes before serving. Allowing the meat to rest in a warm place enables the moisture to re-absorb, resulting in a tender and juicy steak.

>4 For rare, place the steak in a very hot skillet and cook for 1½ minutes on each side to sear the outside but leave the centre pink. Let stand for 3 minutes before serving.

29

>5 For medium, place the steak in a very hot skillet and cook for 2½–3 minutes on each side, so that the outside is cooked and the centre still retains some pinkness. Let stand for 3 minutes before serving.

>6 For medium–well done, place the steak in a very hot skillet and cook for 3–4½ minutes, so that the steak is cooked through with no pink remaining inside. Let stand for 3 minutes before serving.

Serve.

easy roasted chicken

serves 6

ingredients

5-pound chicken

4 tablespoons salted butter, softened

2 tablespoons chopped fresh lemon thyme, plus extra sprigs to garnish

1 lemon, cut into quarters

¼ cup white wine, plus extra if needed

salt and pepper

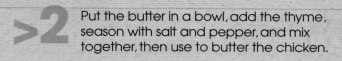

>1 Preheat the oven to 425°F. Place the chicken in a roasting pan.

>2 Put the butter in a bowl, add the thyme, season with salt and pepper, and mix together, then use to butter the chicken.

>3 Place the lemon inside the cavity. Pour the wine over the chicken and roast in the preheated oven for 15 minutes.

>4 Reduce the temperature to 375°F and roast, basting frequently, for an additional 1¾ hours.

33

>5 To check a whole bird is cooked through, pierce the thickest part of the leg between the drumstick and the thigh with the tip of a sharp knife or metal skewer. Any juices should be piping hot and clear with no traces of red or pink. To further check, gently pull the leg away from the body, the leg should "give" and no traces of pinkness or blood should remain. Transfer to a warmed platter, cover with foil and allow to rest for 10 minutes.

>6 Place the roasting pan on the stove and simmer the pan juices gently over low heat until they have reduced and are thick and glossy. Season with salt and pepper and reserve.

>7 To carve the chicken, place on a clean cutting board. Using a carving knife and fork, cut between the wings and the side of the breast. Remove the wings and cut slices off the breast.

>8 Cut the legs from the body and cut through the joint to separate the drumstick and thigh pieces.

Serve with the pan juices, garnished with thyme sprigs.

broiled fish

serves 4

ingredients

olive oil, for brushing
4 white fish fillets, such
   as red snapper, flounder,
   or orange roughy, about
   6 ounces each

salt and pepper
lemon wedges, to serve

>1 Preheat the broiler to its highest setting with a shelf at a level where the fish will be about ½ inch from the heat source. Brush a shallow flameproof dish with oil.

>2 To remove the skin, place the fish skin side down, then slide a sharp knife between the skin and the flesh, keeping the knife flat.

>3 Brush the fish generously with oil and season with salt and pepper. Lay the fish in the prepared dish.

>4 Place under the preheated broiler and cook for 3–4 minutes until the fish becomes opaque.

>5 Using a spatula, carefully turn over the fillets. Brush with oil and sprinkle with salt and pepper.

>6 Broil the other side for 3–4 minutes, depending on thickness, until the fish is firm and flakes easily with a fork.

Serve immediately with lemon wedges.

vegetable pizza

makes 1 pizza

ingredients

2 tablespoons olive oil
1 (12-inch) store-bought
  pizza crust
3 tablespoons
  tomato paste

1 tablespoon chopped
  fresh thyme
1 onion, finely chopped
1 small green bell pepper,
  seeded and thinly sliced
2 tomatoes, sliced

6 ripe black olives, pitted
  and halved
4 ounces mozzarella
  cheese, torn into pieces
salt and pepper

> **1** Preheat the oven to 425°F. Brush a large baking sheet with a little of the oil.

> **2** Place the pizza crust on the prepared baking sheet.

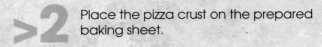

> **3** Spread the tomato paste over the pizza crust to within ¾ inch of the edge.

> **4** Sprinkle with the thyme.

41

>**5** Arrange the onion, green bell pepper, tomatoes, and olives over the pizza.

>**6** Sprinkle with the cheese.

>**7** Season with salt and pepper and drizzle with the remaining oil.

>**8** Bake in the preheated oven for 12–15 minutes, until bubbling and golden.

Serve immediately.

spaghetti & meat sauce

serves 4

ingredients

2 tablespoons olive oil
1 large onion, chopped
1 pound ground beef

1 green bell pepper, seeded
   and chopped
1 garlic clove, crushed
⅔ cup red wine
   or beef stock

1 (14½-ounce) can diced
   plum tomatoes
2 tablespoons tomato
   paste
1 tablespoon dried oregano

8 ounces dried spaghetti
salt and pepper
freshly grated Parmesan
   cheese, to serve

> **1** Heat the oil in a large saucepan over high heat.

> **2** Add the onion and ground beef and fry, stirring until lightly browned with no remaining traces of pink.

> **3** Stir in the green bell pepper and garlic.

> **4** Add the wine, tomatoes, tomato paste, and oregano. Bring to a boil and boil rapidly for 2 minutes.

Reduce the heat, cover, and simmer for 20 minutes, stirring occasionally.

Meanwhile, bring a large saucepan of lightly salted water to a boil, add the spaghetti, bring back to a boil, and cook according to the package directions, until tender but still firm to the bite.

Drain the spaghetti in a colander and return to the pan.

Season the sauce with salt and pepper, then stir into the spaghetti.

Serve immediately, with Parmesan cheese.

pasta pesto

serves 4

ingredients
1 pound dried tagliatelle
salt

pesto
2 garlic cloves
3 tablespoons pine nuts
3 cups fresh basil leaves,
 plus extra to garnish
½ cup olive oil
⅔ cup freshly grated
 Parmesan cheese

 >1 To make the pesto, put the garlic, pine nuts, and a pinch of salt into a food processor and process briefly. Add the basil and process to a paste.

 >2 With the motor still running, gradually add the oil. Scrape into a bowl and beat in the Parmesan cheese. Season with salt.

Divide among warm serving dishes and top with the remaining pesto. Garnish with basil and serve immediately.

>3 Bring a large, heavy saucepan of lightly salted water to a boil. Add the tagliatelle, bring back to a boil, and cook according to the package directions, until tender but still firm to the bite.

>4 Drain well, return to the saucepan, and toss with half the pesto.

perfect potatoes

serves 4

ingredients

baked

4 large russet potatoes,
  scrubbed
salt

roasted

4 large russet potatoes or
  1½ pounds new potatoes
3 tablespoons sunflower oil
salt

mashed

6–9 Yukon gold or russet
  potatoes (about
  1½ pounds)
⅔ cup whole milk
salt and pepper

>1 Baked
Preheat the oven to 400°F. Pierce each potato with a fork to let the steam escape.

>2
Rub some salt into the skins and bake in the preheated oven for 1 hour 15 minutes, until tender. Cut a crosswise slit in each potato.

>1 Roasted
Preheat the oven to 425°F. Peel the potatoes and cut into large, even chunks. Rinse in cold water.

>2
Bring a large saucepan of lightly salted water to a boil. Add the potatoes, bring back to a boil, and cook for 10 minutes. Drain, then shake in the pan.

> **3** Heat the oil in a roasting pan and add the potatoes, turning to coat. Roast in the preheated oven for about 45 minutes, turning occasionally, until golden. Serve immediately.

> **1** **Mashed**
Peel the potatoes and cut into even chunks.

> **2** Bring a large saucepan of lightly salted water to a boil, add the potatoes, bring back to a boil, and cook for 20 minutes, or until tender. Drain well.

> **3** Put the milk in a separate saucepan and heat until almost boiling, then add to the potatoes and mash until smooth using either a fork, handheld masher, or ricer. Season with salt and pepper.

Serve immediately.

roasted vegetables

serves 4–6

ingredients
3 parsnips, cut into 2-inch chunks
4 baby turnips, cut into quarters (optional)
3 carrots, cut into 2-inch chunks
1 pound butternut squash, cut into 2-inch chunks
1 pound sweet potatoes, cut into 2-inch chunks
2 garlic cloves, finely chopped
2 tablespoons chopped fresh rosemary, plus extra to garnish
2 tablespoons chopped fresh thyme, plus extra to garnish
2 teaspoons chopped fresh sage, plus extra to garnish
3 tablespoons olive oil
salt and pepper

>1 Preheat the oven to 425°F. Arrange all the vegetables in a single layer in a large roasting pan.

>2 Sprinkle with the garlic and the herbs. Pour the oil over the vegetables and season well with salt and pepper.

Serve with a good handful of fresh herbs sprinkled over the top and a final sprinkling of salt and pepper.

>3 Toss together all the ingredients until they are well mixed and coated with the oil (if you have time you can let them marinate so the flavors are absorbed).

>4 Roast the vegetables at the top of the preheated oven for 50–60 minutes, until they are cooked and browned. Turn the vegetables over halfway through the cooking time.

easy rice & peas

serves 4

ingredients

2 tablespoons olive oil
1 onion, sliced
1 garlic clove, crushed
1 tablespoon chopped
  thyme

1¾ cups vegetable stock
1 cup long-grain rice
¼ cup coconut milk
1 (15-ounce) can red
  kidney beans, drained
  and rinsed

salt and pepper
fresh thyme sprigs, to garnish

>1 Heat the oil in a large saucepan, add the onion, and cook over medium heat, stirring, for about 5 minutes, until soft.

>2 Add the garlic and thyme and cook, stirring, for 30 seconds.

>3 Stir the stock into the pan and bring to a boil.

>4 Stir in the rice, then reduce the heat, cover, and simmer for 12–15 minutes, until the rice is just tender.

5 Stir in the coconut milk and beans, then season with salt and pepper.

6 Cook gently for 2–3 minutes, stirring occasionally, until thoroughly heated.

Serve hot, garnished with thyme.

coleslaw

serves 4

ingredients
3½ cups shredded green
  cabbage
1 carrot, peeled and grated
4 scallions, thinly sliced
2 tablespoons finely
  chopped fresh parsley

dressing
¼ cup mayonnaise
2 tablespoons sour cream
  or crème fraîche
1 teaspoon whole-grain
  mustard
1 tablespoon lemon juice
salt and pepper

>1 Combine all the vegetables in a large bowl.

>2 Add the parsley and stir to mix evenly.

60

Serve.

>3 To make the dressing, stir together the mayonnaise, sour cream, mustard, and lemon juice. Season with salt and pepper.

>4 Spoon the dressing into the vegetables. Toss well to mix evenly. Adjust the seasoning to taste.

mixed berry tarts

serves 6

ingredients

1 sheet rolled dough
  pie crust
8 ounces mascarpone
  cheese
1 teaspoon vanilla extract

1 tablespoon honey
3½ cups mixed berries,
  such as strawberries,
  raspberries, red currants,
  and blueberries

confectioners' sugar,
  for dusting

Preheat the oven to 400°F. Unroll the dough onto a work surface and cut into six squares.

>2 Place each dough square in a 4-inch loose-bottom tart pan and ease gently into the pan, without stretching.

>3 Roll a rolling pin over the top of the pans to trim the excess dough. Press the dough into the fluted sides with your fingers.

>4 Place the pans on a baking sheet and prick the shell bottoms with a fork. Press parchment paper into each dough-lined pan and add dried beans.

Bake in the preheated oven for 10 minutes, remove the paper and weights, and bake for 5 minutes. Let cool in the pans for 10 minutes.

Carefully remove the tart shells from the pans and let cool completely on a wire rack.

> 7 Mix the mascarpone cheese with the vanilla extract and honey, then spoon into the tarts and spread evenly.

> 8 Hull and halve the strawberries and mix with the remaining fruits, then divide among the tarts.

Dust the tarts with sifted confectioners' sugar
just before serving.

vanilla-frosted cupcakes

makes 12

ingredients

1 stick salted butter,
  softened
½ cup granulated sugar
2 eggs, lightly beaten

1 cup all-purpose flour
  mixed with 1½ teaspoons
  baking powder
1 tablespoon milk
1 tablespoon sprinkles

frosting

1½ sticks unsalted butter,
  softened
1 teaspoon vanilla extract
2¼ cups confectioners'
  sugar, sifted

>**1** Preheat the oven to 350°F. Put 12 paper cupcake liners in a muffin pan, or put 12 double-layer paper cupcake liners on a baking sheet.

>**2** Put the butter and sugar in a bowl. Beat together until light and fluffy.

>**3** Gradually beat in the eggs. Sift in the flour and baking powder and fold in with the milk.

>**4** Spoon the mixture into the cupcake liners. Bake in the preheated oven for 20 minutes, until golden brown and firm to the touch. Transfer to a wire rack to cool.

perfect pancakes

serves 4

ingredients

1¼ cups all-purpose flour
1½ teaspoons baking
  powder
pinch of salt
2 tablespoons granulated
  sugar

1 cup whole milk
1 extra-large egg
2 tablespoons sunflower oil,
  plus extra for greasing
1 cup blueberries, plus extra
  to serve

whipped butter

1 stick unsalted butter, at
  room temperature
2 tablespoons milk
1 tablespoon maple syrup,
  plus extra to serve

> **1** To make the whipped butter, place the butter in a bowl and beat with an electric mixer until soft.

> **2** Add the milk and maple syrup and beat hard until pale and fluffy.

> **3** To make the pancakes, sift the flour, baking powder, salt, and sugar into a bowl.

> **4** Add the milk, egg, and oil and whisk to a smooth batter.

>5 Stir in the blueberries and let stand for 5 minutes.

>6 Lightly grease a flat griddle pan or skillet and heat over medium heat. Spoon tablespoons of batter onto the pan and cook until bubbles appear on the surface.

>7 Turn over with a spatula and cook the other side until golden brown.

>8 Repeat this process using the remaining batter, while keeping the cooked pancakes warm in an oven at low heat.

Serve the pancakes in stacks with extra
blueberries, a spoonful of whipped butter,
and a drizzle of maple syrup.

quick tomato soup

serves 4

ingredients
2 tablespoons olive oil
1 large onion, chopped
1 (14½-ounce) can peeled
   plum tomatoes
1¼ cups chicken stock or
   vegetable stock
1 tablespoon tomato paste
1 teaspoon hot chili sauce
handful of fresh basil leaves
salt and pepper

>1 Heat the oil in a large saucepan over medium heat, then add the onion and sauté for 4–5 minutes, stirring, until soft.

>2 Add the tomatoes with their can juices, stock, tomato paste, chili sauce, and half the basil leaves.

Serve the soup in warm serving bowls,
garnished with the remaining basil leaves.

>3 Puree with an electric blender until smooth,
then transfer to the pan.

>4 Stir the soup over medium heat
until just boiling, then season with
salt and pepper.

caesar salad

serves 4

ingredients

½ cup olive oil

2 garlic cloves

5 slices white bread, crusts removed, cut into ½-inch cubes

1 egg

3 Romaine lettuce

2 tablespoons lemon juice

8 canned anchovy fillets, drained and coarsely chopped

salt and pepper

fresh Parmesan cheese shavings, to serve

> **1** Heat ¼ cup of the oil in a heavy skillet. Add the garlic and bread and cook, stirring frequently, for 4–5 minutes, until the bread is crisp and golden.

> **2** Remove the croutons from the skillet with a slotted spoon and drain on paper towels.

> **3** Meanwhile, bring a small saucepan of water to a boil. Add the egg and cook for 1 minute, then remove from the pan and set aside.

> **4** Arrange the lettuce leaves in a bowl. In a separate bowl, add the remaining oil and the lemon juice, season with salt and pepper, and mix together.

>5 Crack the egg into the dressing and beat to blend. Pour the dressing over the lettuce and toss well.

>6 Add the chopped anchovies and croutons, discarding the garlic, and toss the salad again.

Sprinkle with Parmesan cheese shavings and serve.

basic beef stew

serves 4

ingredients

3 pounds boneless
 chuck steak, cut into
 2-inch pieces
2 tablespoons vegetable oil
2 onions, cut into
 1-inch pieces

3 tablespoons
 all-purpose flour
3 garlic cloves, finely
 chopped
4 cups beef stock

3 carrots, cut into
 1-inch lengths
2 celery stalks, cut into
 1-inch lengths
1 tablespoon ketchup
1 bay leaf

¼ teaspoon dried thyme
¼ teaspoon dried rosemary
8 white round or Yukon gold
 potatoes, scrubbed and
 cut into large chunks
salt and pepper

>1 Season the steak generously with salt and pepper. Heat the oil in a large stockpot, dutch oven, or flameproof casserole dish over high heat.

>2 When the oil begins to smoke, add the steak and cook, stirring frequently, for 5–8 minutes, until well browned. Using a slotted spoon, transfer to a bowl.

>3 Reduce the heat to medium, add the onions to the pot, and cook, stirring occasionally, for 5 minutes, until translucent.

>4 Stir in the flour and cook, stirring continuously, for 2 minutes. Add the garlic and cook for 1 minute.

hamburgers

serves 4

ingredients

1½ pounds fresh
  ground beef
1 red bell pepper, seeded
  and finely chopped
1 garlic clove, finely
  chopped
2 small red chiles, seeded
  and finely chopped
1 tablespoon chopped
  fresh basil
½ teaspoon ground cumin
salt and pepper
fresh basil sprigs, to garnish
burger buns, to serve

> **>1** Preheat the broiler to medium–high. Put
> the beef, red bell pepper, garlic, chiles,
> chopped basil, and cumin into a bowl.

> **>2** Mix until well combined and season
> with salt and pepper.

Garnish with basil sprigs and serve immediately in burger buns.

>3 Using your hands, form the mixture into four patty shapes. Place the patties under the preheated broiler and cook for 5–8 minutes.

>4 Using a spatula, turn the burgers and cook on the other side for 5–8 minutes. To check the burgers are cooked through, cut into the middle to check that the meat is no longer pink. Any juices that run out should be clear and piping hot with visible steam rising.

>5 Place the chicken in a shallow ovenproof dish and arrange the tomatoes around it.

>6 Season with salt and pepper, pour the wine over the chicken, and drizzle with the oil.

>7 Bake in the preheated oven for 15–20 minutes. To check that the meat is cooked through, cut into the middle to check that there are no remaining traces of pink or red. Any juices that run out should be clear and piping hot with visible steam rising.

>8 Cut the chicken breasts in half diagonally, place on serving plates with the tomatoes, and spoon the juices over them.

Serve the chicken with chunks of ciabatta.

grilled turkey cutlets with lemon

serves 4

ingredients

1 lemon
2 tablespoons olive oil
1 garlic clove, crushed

4 turkey cutlets
salt and pepper
salad, to serve

1 Finely grate the rind from the lemon and squeeze the juice.

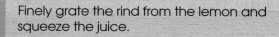 **2** Mix together the lemon juice, oil, and garlic in a wide, nonmetallic dish.

3 Place the turkey cutlets in the lemon mixture, turning to coat evenly. Cover with plastic wrap and chill in the refrigerator for 30 minutes. Drain the turkey, discarding the marinade, and season with salt and pepper.

4 Heat a ridged grill pan over high heat. Place the turkey cutlets in the pan, and cook for about 4 minutes, until golden, before turning over with a pair of tongs or a spatula.

>5 Using tongs, turn the turkey breasts over and cook for a further 3–4 minutes. To check that the meat is cooked through, cut into the middle to check that there are no remaining traces of pink or red. Any juices that run out should be clear and piping hot with visible steam rising.

>6 Transfer the turkey to a warm plate, cover with aluminum foil, and let stand for 3–4 minutes before serving.

Serve with salad.

steamed salmon

serves 4

ingredients
3 tablespoons butter,
   melted
4 salmon fillets, about
   5 ounces each
finely grated rind and juice
   of 1 lemon
1 tablespoon snipped
   chives
1 tablespoon chopped
   parsley
salt and pepper
salad and crusty bread,
   to serve

>**1** Preheat the oven to 400°F. Cut four 12-inch squares of double thickness aluminum foil and brush with the melted butter.

>**2** Place a piece of salmon on each square and spoon the lemon rind and juice over the fish. Sprinkle with the chives, parsley, salt, and pepper.

Transfer the salmon and juices to warm serving plates and serve immediately with salad and crusty bread.

>3 Wrap the foil over loosely and seal firmly with the seam on top.

>4 Place the packages on a baking pan and bake for 20 minutes, or until the fish flakes easily.

>5 Add three-quarters of the cheddar cheese and all the Parmesan cheese and stir through until they have melted in. Season with salt and pepper and remove from the heat.

>6 Preheat the broiler to high. Put the macaroni into a shallow heatproof dish, then pour the sauce over the pasta.

>7 Sprinkle the remaining cheese over the top and place the dish under the preheated broiler.

>8 Broil until the cheese begins to brown.

mushroom stroganoff

serves 4

ingredients
2 tablespoons butter
1 onion, finely chopped
6½ cups quartered white
   button mushrooms
   (about 1 pound)
1 teaspoon tomato paste
1 teaspoon whole-grain
   mustard
⅔ cup crème fraîche
   or sour cream
1 teaspoon paprika, plus
   extra to garnish
salt and pepper
fresh flat-leaf parsley sprigs,
   to garnish

>1 Heat the butter in a large, heavy skillet. Add the onion and cook gently for 5–10 minutes, until soft.

>2 Add the mushrooms to the skillet and sauté for a few minutes, until they begin to soften.

Garnish with extra paprika and parsley sprigs and serve immediately.

>3 Stir in the tomato paste and mustard, then add the crème fraîche. Cook gently, stirring continuously, for 5 minutes.

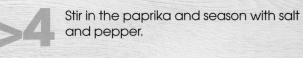

>4 Stir in the paprika and season with salt and pepper.

raspberry muffins

makes 12

ingredients

2¼ cups all-purpose flour
1 tablespoon baking
  powder
⅔ cup granulated sugar
2 eggs

⅔ cup milk
½ cup sunflower oil
1 teaspoon vanilla extract
rind and juice of 1 small
  lemon

1 cup fresh raspberries
confectioners' sugar, for
  sprinkling

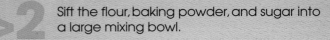

>**1** Preheat the oven to 400°F. Place 12 muffin cups in a muffin pan.

>**2** Sift the flour, baking powder, and sugar into a large mixing bowl.

>**3** Put the eggs, milk, oil, vanilla extract, and lemon rind and juice in a separate mixing bowl and beat together with a fork.

>**4** Stir the wet mixture into the dry ingredients and mix lightly and evenly to make a soft batter.

> **5** Add the raspberries to the batter, stirring lightly until just combined.

> **6** Spoon the batter into the muffin cups. Bake in the preheated oven for about 20 minutes, until firm and golden.

Let cool on a wire rack or serve slightly warm, sprinkled with a little confectioners' sugar.

chocolate chip cookies

makes 30

ingredients

1⅓ cups all-purpose flour
1 teaspoon baking powder
½ cup soft margarine, plus
  extra for greasing
⅓ cup firmly packed
  light brown sugar
¼ cup granulated sugar
½ teaspoon vanilla extract
1 egg
¾ cup semsiweet dark
  chocolate chips

> **1** Preheat the oven to 375°F. Lightly grease two baking sheets.

> **2** Place all of the ingredients in a large mixing bowl and beat until well combined.

Serve immediately or store in an airtight container.

>3 Place tablespoonfuls of the dough on the prepared baking sheets, spacing them well apart to allow for spreading during cooking.

>4 Bake in the preheated oven for 10–12 minutes, or until the cookies are golden brown. Using a spatula, transfer the cookies to a wire rack to cool completely.

113

> **5** Stir the broken cookies, marshmallows, and nuts into the chocolate mixture.

> **6** Pour the chocolate batter into the lined pan, pressing down with the back of a spoon. Chill in the refrigerator for at least 2 hours, or until firm.

> **7** Carefully invert out of the pan onto a wooden board.

> **8** Dust with confectioners' sugar.

Cut into eight pieces to serve.

strawberry ice cream sundae

serves 4

ingredients

1 pint strawberries, hulled
2 tablespoons
  confectioners' sugar
1 tablespoon lemon juice
⅔ cup heavy cream
2 cups vanilla
  ice cream
¼ cup chopped blanched
  almonds, toasted

>1 Place about one-third of the strawberries in a bowl with the sugar and lemon juice and puree with an electric mixer until smooth.

>2 Rub the puree through a fine strainer into a bowl, and discard the seeds.

Serve immediately.

>3 Whip the cream until thick enough to hold soft peaks. Slice the remaining strawberries. Layer the strawberries, scoops of ice cream, and spoonfuls of cream in four glasses.

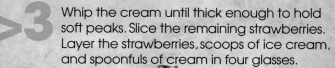

>4 Spoon the sauce over the sundaes and sprinkle with chopped almonds.

intermediate

cream of chicken soup

serves 4

ingredients

3 tablespoons butter
4 shallots, chopped
1 leek, sliced
1 pound skinless, boneless
  chicken breasts, chopped

2½ cups chicken stock
1 tablespoon chopped
  fresh parsley
1 tablespoon chopped
  fresh thyme, plus extra
  sprigs to garnish

¾ cup heavy cream
salt and pepper

>1 Melt the butter in a large saucepan over medium heat. Add the shallots and cook, stirring, for 3 minutes, until slightly softened.

>2 Add the leek and cook for 25 minutes until the chicken is cooked through.

>3 Add the chicken, stock and herbs, and season with salt and pepper. Bring to a boil, then reduce the heat and simmer for 25 minutes. To check that the meat is cooked through, cut into the middle to check that there are no remaining traces of pink or red. Any juices that run out should be clear and piping hot with visible steam rising.

>4 Remove from the heat and let cool for 10 minutes. Transfer the soup to a food processor or blender and process until smooth (you may need to do this in batches).

>5 Return the soup to the rinsed-out pan and warm over low heat for 5 minutes.

>6 Stir in the cream and cook for an additional 2 minutes, then remove from the heat and ladle into serving bowls.

Garnish with thyme sprigs and
serve immediately.

minestrone soup

serves 4

ingredients

2 tablespoons olive oil
2 garlic cloves, chopped
2 red onions, chopped
3 ounces prosciutto, sliced
1 red bell pepper and
  1 orange bell pepper,
  seeded and chopped
1 (14½-ounce) can
  diced tomatoes
4 cups vegetable stock
1 celery stalk, chopped
1 (15-ounce) can cranberry
  beans, rinsed and drained
1 cup shredded green
  cabbage
½ cup frozen peas
1 tablespoon chopped
  fresh parsley
3 ounces dried vermicelli pasta
salt and pepper
freshly grated Parmesan
  cheese, to serve

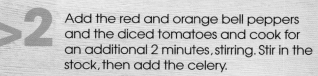

> **1** Heat the oil in a large saucepan. Add the garlic, onions, and prosciutto and cook over medium heat, stirring, for 3 minutes, until slightly softened.

> **2** Add the red and orange bell peppers and the diced tomatoes and cook for an additional 2 minutes, stirring. Stir in the stock, then add the celery.

Sprinkle with the Parmesan cheese and serve immediately.

>3 Add the beans to the pan with the cabbage, peas, and parsley. Season with salt and pepper. Bring to a boil, then reduce the heat and simmer for 30 minutes.

>4 Add the pasta to the pan. Cook according to the pasta's package directions. Remove from the heat and ladle into bowls.

meatloaf

serves 6–8

ingredients

2 tablespoons butter
1 tablespoon olive oil, plus extra for brushing
3 garlic cloves, chopped
2 carrots, finely diced
1 celery stalk, finely diced
1 onion, finely diced

1 red bell pepper, seeded and finely diced
4 large white mushrooms, finely diced
1 teaspoon dried thyme
2 teaspoons finely chopped rosemary

1 teaspoon Worcestershire sauce
⅓ cup ketchup
½ teaspoon cayenne pepper
2½ pounds ground beef, chilled

2 eggs, beaten
1 cup fresh breadcrumbs
2 tablespoons packed brown sugar
1 tablespoon Dijon mustard
salt and pepper

128

>1 Melt the butter with the oil and garlic in a large skillet. Add the vegetables and cook over medium heat, stirring frequently, for 10 minutes, until most of the moisture has evaporated.

>2 Remove from the heat and stir in the herbs, Worcestershire sauce, ¼ cup of the ketchup, and the cayenne pepper. Let cool.

>3 Preheat the oven to 325°F. Brush a loaf pan with oil.

>4 Put the beef into a large bowl and gently break it up with your fingertips. Add the vegetable mixture and eggs, season with salt and pepper, and mix gently with your fingers. Add the breadcrumbs and mix.

>5 Transfer the meatloaf mixture to the loaf pan. Smooth the surface and bake in the preheated oven for 30 minutes.

>6 Meanwhile, make a glaze by beating together the sugar, the remaining 2 tablespoons of ketchup, the mustard, and a pinch of salt.

>7 Remove the meatloaf from the oven and spread the glaze evenly over the top. Return to the oven and bake for a further 35–45 minutes. To check the meatloaf is cooked through, cut into the middle to check that the meat is no longer pink. Any juices that run out should be clear and piping hot with visible steam rising.

>8 Remove from the oven and let rest for at least 15 minutes.

Slice thickly to serve.

meatballs

serves 4

ingredients

1 tablespoon olive oil
1 small onion, finely
  chopped
2 garlic cloves, finely
  chopped
2 fresh thyme sprigs, finely
  chopped

1½ pounds fresh ground
  beef
½ cup fresh breadcrumbs
1 egg, lightly beaten
salt and pepper

sauce

1 onion, cut into wedges
3 red bell peppers, halved
  and seeded
1 (14½-ounce) can diced
  tomatoes
1 bay leaf

> **1** Heat the oil in a skillet. Add the onion and garlic and cook over a low heat for 5 minutes, or until soft. Place in a bowl with the thyme, ground beef, breadcrumbs, and egg. Season to taste with salt and pepper, mix thoroughly and shape into 20 golf-ball sized balls.

> **2** Heat a large skillet over low–medium heat. Add the meatballs and cook, stirring gently for 15 minutes. To check that the meat is cooked through, cut into the middle to check that there are no remaining traces of pink.

> **3** Meanwhile, to make the sauce, cook the onion wedges and red bell pepper halves under the preheated broiler, turning frequently, for 10 minutes, until the pepper skins are blistered and charred.

> **4** Put the bell peppers into a plastic bag, tie the top, and let cool. Set the onion wedges aside. Peel off the pepper skins and coarsely chop the flesh.

Put the bell pepper flesh into a food processor with the onion wedges and tomatoes. Process to a smooth puree and season with salt and pepper.

>6 Pour into a saucepan with the bay leaf and bring to a boil. Reduce the heat and simmer, stirring occasionally, for 10 minutes. Remove and discard the bay leaf.

Serve the sauce immediately with
the meatballs.

pot roast

serves 6

ingredients

4–5 white round or Yukon gold potatoes, cut into large chunks

2½ tablespoons all-purpose flour

3½-pound rolled brisket joint

2 tablespoons vegetable oil

2 tablespoons butter

1 onion, finely chopped

2 celery stalks, diced

2 carrots, peeled and diced

1 teaspoon dill seed

1 teaspoon dried thyme

1½ cups red wine

⅓–½ cup beef stock

salt and pepper

2 tablespoons chopped fresh dill, to serve

>1 Bring a large saucepan of lightly salted water to a boil. Add the potatoes, bring back to a boil, and cook for 10 minutes. Drain and set aside.

>2 Preheat the oven to 275°F. Mix 2 tablespoons of the flour with 1 teaspoon salt and ¼ teaspoon pepper in a large shallow dish. Dip the meat in the flour to coat.

>3 Heat the oil in a flameproof casserole dish or dutch oven, add the meat, and brown. Transfer to a plate. Add half the butter to the dish, then add the onion, celery, carrots, dill seed, and thyme and cook for 5 minutes.

>4 Return the meat and juices to the casserole dish. Pour in the wine and enough stock to reach one-third of the way up the meat and bring to a boil.

>5 Cover and cook in the oven for 3 hours, turning the meat every 30 minutes. Add the potatoes and more stock, if necessary, after 2 hours.

>6 When ready, transfer the meat and vegetables to a warm serving dish. Strain the cooking liquid to remove any solids, then return the liquid to the casserole dish.

>7 Mix the remaining butter and flour to a paste.

>8 Bring the cooking liquid to a boil. Beat in small pieces of the flour and butter paste, beating continuously until the sauce is smooth.

Pour the sauce over the meat and
vegetables. Sprinkle with fresh dill and serve.

pork chops with applesauce

serves 4

ingredients
4 pork rib chops on the
  bone, each about
  1¼ inches thick,
  at room temperature
1½ tablespoons sunflower oil
salt and pepper

applesauce
3 cooking apples, such as
  Granny Smith, peeled,
  cored, and diced
¼ cup granulated sugar
finely grated zest of
  ½ lemon
½ tablespoon lemon juice
¼ cup water
¼ teaspoon ground
  cinnamon
pat of butter

>1 Preheat the oven to 400°F. To make the
applesauce, put the first five ingredients
into a heavy saucepan over high heat
and bring to a boil, stirring.

>2 Reduce the heat to low, cover, and
simmer for 15–20 minutes, until the
apples are soft. Add the cinnamon
and butter and beat until you have the
desired consistency. Remove from the
heat, cover, and keep warm.

Transfer the chops to warm plates and spoon the pan juices over them. Serve immediately, with the applesauce.

>3 Meanwhile, season the chops with salt and pepper. Heat the oil in a large ovenproof skillet over medium–high heat. Add the chops and cook for 3 minutes on each side.

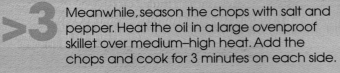

>4 Transfer the pan to the preheated oven and roast the chops for 7–9 minutes. To check that the meat is cooked through, cut into the middle to check that there are no remaining traces of pink or red. Any juices that run out should be clear and piping hot with visible steam rising.

chicken fajitas

serves 4

ingredients

3 tablespoons olive oil, plus
  extra for drizzling
3 tablespoons maple syrup
  or honey
1 tablespoon red wine
  vinegar
2 garlic cloves, crushed
2 teaspoons dried oregano
1–2 teaspoons crushed
  red pepper
4 skinless, boneless chicken
  breasts
2 red bell peppers, seeded
  and cut into 1-inch strips
salt and pepper
warm flour tortillas and
  shredded lettuce, to serve

>1 Place the oil, maple syrup, vinegar, garlic, oregano, and crushed red pepper, in a large, shallow dish, season with salt and pepper, and mix together.

>2 Slice the chicken across the grain into slices 1 inch thick. Toss in the marinade to coat. Cover and chill for 2–3 hours, turning occasionally.

142

Divide the chicken and bell peppers among the flour tortillas, top with a little shredded lettuce, wrap, and serve immediately.

>3 Drain the chicken. Heat a griddle pan until hot. Add the chicken and cook over medium–high heat for 3–4 minutes on each side. To check that the meat is cooked through, cut into the middle to check that there are no remaining traces of pink or red. Transfer to a warmed plate.

>4 Add the bell peppers, skin side down, to the pan and cook for 2 minutes on each side, until cooked through. Transfer to the plate with the chicken.

turkey stir-fry

serves 4

ingredients

1 pound turkey breast,
  skinned and cut into strips
1 cup long-grain rice
1 tablespoon vegetable oil
1 head broccoli,
  cut into florets

2 heads bok choy, washed
  and separated
1 red bell pepper, seeded
  and thinly sliced
¼ cup chicken stock
salt

marinade
1 tablespoon soy sauce
1 tablespoon honey
2 garlic cloves, crushed

> **1** To make the marinade, combine the ingredients in a medium bowl. Add the turkey and toss to coat. Cover with plastic wrap and marinate in the refrigerator for 2 hours.

> **2** Cook the rice in a saucepan of lightly salted water according to the package directions. Drain and keep warm.

> **3** Meanwhile, preheat a wok over medium–high heat, add the oil, and heat for 1 minute. Add the turkey and stir-fry for 3 minutes. To check that the meat is cooked through, cut into the middle to check that there are no remaining traces of pink or red. Any juices that run out should be clear and piping hot with visible steam rising.

> **4** Remove the turkey with a slotted spoon, set aside, and keep warm. Add the broccoli, bok choy, and red pepper to the wok and stir-fry for 2 minutes.

145

>5 Add the stock and continue to stir-fry for 2 minutes, or until the vegetables are tender but still firm to the bite.

>6 Return the turkey to the wok and cook briefly to reheat.

Serve immediately with the rice.

tuna pasta casserole

serves 4

ingredients
8 ounces dried
  elbow macaroni
2 (5-ounce) cans chunk
  light tuna in oil, drained
  and flaked
1 small red onion, grated
2 tablespoons chopped
  fresh parsley
2 cups shredded
  cheddar cheese,
1 extra-large egg, beaten
1 cup light cream
¼ teaspoon grated nutmeg
salt and pepper

> **>1** Preheat the oven to 425°F and place a baking sheet on the middle shelf to heat. Bring a saucepan of lightly salted water to a boil, add the macaroni, and cook according to the package directions, or until tender but still firm to the bite. Drain.

> **>2** Combine the macaroni, tuna, onion, parsley, and half the cheese in a shallow, 1-quart ovenproof dish, spreading evenly.

Serve hot.

> **>3** Add the egg, cream, and nutmeg to a bowl, season with salt and pepper, and beat together. Pour the egg mixture over the pasta and sprinkle with the remaining cheese.

> **>4** Place the dish on the preheated baking sheet in the oven and bake for about 15 minutes, until golden brown and bubbling.

salmon croquettes

makes 8

ingredients

3 russet or Yukon gold
  potatoes, peeled and
  quartered
10 ounces cooked salmon,
  flaked
½ cup chopped fresh dill,
  plus extra to garnish
6 scallions, some green parts
  included, finely chopped

1 tablespoon cornstarch,
  sifted
1 teaspoon salt
½ teaspoon pepper
2 eggs, lightly beaten
flour, for dusting
oil, for frying

garlic mayonnaise

3 large garlic cloves
1 teaspoon sea salt flakes
2 egg yolks, at room
  temperature
1 cup extra virgin olive oil
2 tablespoons lemon juice

> 1 Bring a large saucepan of water to a boil, add the potatoes, bring back to a boil, and cook for 20 minutes, or until tender. Drain well, mash, and set aside.

> 2 Line a baking sheet with parchment paper. Put the salmon, potato, dill, and scallions into a large bowl and lightly mix with a fork.

> 3 Sprinkle with the cornstarch, salt, and pepper. Stir in the eggs.

> 4 With floured hands, form the mixture into 8 patties about ¾ inch thick.

>5 Place the salmon patties on the lined baking sheet and chill for at least 2 hours.

>6 To make the garlic mayonnaise, use a mortar and pestle to crush the garlic and salt to a smooth paste. Transfer to a large bowl. Beat in the egg yolks.

>7 Add the oil, a few drops at a time, beating continuously, until thick and smooth. Beat in the lemon juice. Cover with plastic wrap and set aside.

>8 Heat the oil in a skillet and cook the croquettes over medium–high heat for 8 minutes, until golden. Turn and cook the other side for 4–5 minutes, until golden.

Garnish with dill and serve immediately
with the garlic mayonnaise.

bean burgers

makes 4

ingredients

1 tablespoon sunflower oil, plus extra for brushing

1 onion, finely chopped

1 garlic clove, finely chopped

1 teaspoon ground coriander

1 teaspoon ground cumin

1⅔ cups finely chopped button mushrooms

1 (15-ounce) can red kidney beans, drained and rinsed

2 tablespoons chopped fresh flat-leaf parsley

all-purpose flour, for dusting

salt and pepper

burger buns and lettuce, to serve

> **1** Heat the oil in a heavy skillet over medium heat. Add the onion and cook, stirring frequently, for 5 minutes, or until soft.

> **2** Add the garlic, coriander, and cumin and cook, stirring, for an additional minute.

> **3** Add the mushrooms and cook, stirring frequently, for 4–5 minutes, until all the liquid has evaporated. Transfer to a bowl.

> **4** Put the beans into a bowl and mash with a vegetable masher. Stir into the mushroom mixture with the parsley and season with salt and pepper.

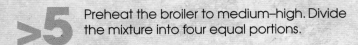

>5 Preheat the broiler to medium–high. Divide the mixture into four equal portions.

>6 Lightly dust with flour and shape into flat patties. Brush with oil and cook under the broiler for 4–5 minutes on each side.

Serve in the burger buns with the lettuce.

pasta arrabbiata

serves 4

ingredients

⅓ cup extra virgin olive oil
8 plum tomatoes, diced
⅔ cup dry white wine
1 tablespoon sun-dried
  tomato paste
2 fresh red chiles
2 garlic cloves, finely
  chopped
¼ cup chopped fresh
  flat-leaf parsley
14 ounces dried penne
salt and pepper
fresh pecorino cheese
  shavings, to garnish

>1 Heat the oil in a skillet over high heat until almost smoking. Add the tomatoes and cook, stirring frequently, for 2–3 minutes.

>2 Reduce the heat to low and cook for about 20 minutes. Season with salt and pepper. Using a wooden spoon, press through a nonmetallic strainer into a saucepan.

Sprinkle with the remaining parsley, garnish with cheese shavings, and serve immediately.

>3 Add the wine, tomato paste, whole chiles, and garlic to the pan and bring to a boil. Reduce the heat and simmer gently, then remove the chiles. Check and adjust the seasoning, adding the chiles back in for a hotter sauce, then stir in half the parsley.

>4 Meanwhile, bring a large saucepan of lightly salted water to a boil. Add the pasta, bring back to a boil, and cook according to the package directions, or until tender but still firm to the bite. Add the sauce to the pasta and toss to coat.

chocolate layer cake

serves 8

ingredients

1¼ cups all-purpose flour
¼ cup unsweetened
  cocoa powder
1 cup granulated sugar
1 tablespoon baking
  powder

1½ sticks unsalted butter, at
  room temperature, plus
  extra for greasing
3 eggs, beaten
1 teaspoon vanilla extract
2 tablespoons whole milk

frosting

1 stick unsalted butter, at
  room temperature
1⅔ cups
  confectioners' sugar
2 tablespoons unsweetened
  cocoa powder
1 teaspoon vanilla extract

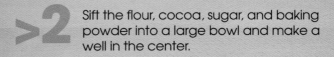

> **1** Preheat the oven to 350°F. Grease and line the bottom and sides of two 8-inch cake pans.

> **2** Sift the flour, cocoa, sugar, and baking powder into a large bowl and make a well in the center.

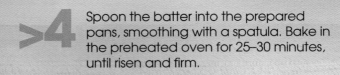

> **3** Beat the butter until soft. Add to the dry ingredients with the eggs, vanilla extract, and milk. Beat lightly with a wooden spoon until just smooth.

> **4** Spoon the batter into the prepared pans, smoothing with a spatula. Bake in the preheated oven for 25–30 minutes, until risen and firm.

>5 Let the cakes cool in the pans for 2–3 minutes, then invert onto a wire rack and let cool completely.

>6 To make the frosting, beat the butter until smooth and fluffy. Sift the confectioners' sugar with the cocoa and beat into the butter until smooth.

>7 Stir in the vanilla extract with enough hot water to mix to a soft spreading consistency.

>8 When the cakes are cold, sandwich them together with half the frosting, then spread the remainder over the top, swirling with a spatula.

Cut into slices and serve.

mini apple crisps

serves 4

ingredients
2 large cooking apples,
 such as Granny Smith,
 peeled, cored, and
 chopped
3 tablespoons maple syrup
juice of ½ lemon
½ teaspoon ground allspice
4 tablespoons unsalted
 butter
1 cup rolled oats
¼ cup firmly packed
 light brown sugar

> **>1** Preheat the oven to 425°F. Place a baking sheet in the oven to heat. Put the apples into a saucepan and stir in the maple syrup, lemon juice, and allspice.

> **>2** Bring to a boil over high heat, then reduce the heat to medium, cover the pan, and cook for 5 minutes, or until almost tender.

Serve the crisps warm.

>3 Meanwhile, melt the butter in a separate saucepan, then remove from the heat and stir in the oats and sugar.

>4 Divide the apples among four 1-cup ovenproof dishes. Sprinkle with the oat mixture. Place on the baking sheet in the preheated oven and bake for 10 minutes, until lightly browned and bubbling.

advanced

lasagna

serves 4

ingredients

2 tablespoons olive oil
2 ounces pancetta, chopped
1 onion, chopped
1 garlic clove, finely chopped

8 ounces fresh ground beef
2 celery stalks, chopped
2 carrots, chopped
pinch of sugar
½ teaspoon dried oregano

1 (14½-ounce) can diced tomatoes
2 teaspoons Dijon mustard
2 cups store-bought cheese sauce

8 ounces oven-ready lasagna noodles
1½ cups freshly grated Parmesan cheese, plus extra for sprinkling
salt and pepper

>1 Preheat the oven to 375°F. Heat the oil in a large, heavy saucepan. Add the pancetta and cook over medium heat, stirring occasionally, for 3 minutes.

>2 Add the onion and garlic and cook, stirring occasionally, for 5 minutes, or until soft.

>3 Add the ground beef and cook, breaking it up with a wooden spoon, until brown all over with no remaining traces of pink. Stir in the celery and carrots and cook for 5 minutes.

>4 Season with salt and pepper. Add the sugar, oregano, and tomatoes and their can juices. Bring to a boil, reduce the heat, and simmer for 30 minutes.

> **5** Meanwhile, stir the mustard into the cheese sauce.

> **6** In a large, rectangular ovenproof dish, make alternate layers of meat sauce, lasagna noodles, and Parmesan cheese.

> **7** Pour the cheese sauce over the layers, covering them completely, and sprinkle with Parmesan cheese.

> **8** Bake in the preheated oven for 30 minutes, or until golden brown and bubbling.

Serve immediately.

burritos

serves 4

ingredients

1 tablespoon olive oil
1 onion, chopped
1 garlic clove, finely
  chopped
1 pound fresh ground beef
3 large tomatoes, seeded
  and diced

1 red bell pepper, seeded
  and chopped
4 cups mixed rinsed, drained
  canned beans, such as
  kidney beans, pinto beans,
  and chickpeas
½ cup vegetable stock

1 tablespoon finely
  chopped fresh parsley
8 whole-wheat flour tortillas
½ cup tomato paste
½ cup shredded
  cheddar cheese,
3 scallions, sliced

sea salt and pepper
mixed lettuce, to serve

> **1** Heat the oil in a large, nonstick skillet, add the onion and garlic, and cook until the onion is soft but not brown. Remove from the skillet.

> **2** Add the ground beef and cook over a high heat, breaking it up with a wooden spoon, until brown all over with no remaining traces of pink. Drain off any excess oil.

> **3** Return the onion and garlic to the skillet, add the tomatoes and red bell pepper, and cook for 8–10 minutes.

> **4** Add the mixed beans, stock, and parsley, season with salt and pepper, and cook, uncovered, for an additional 20–30 minutes, until well thickened.

>5 Meanwhile, preheat the oven to 350°F. Mash the meat mixture to break up the beans, then divide among the tortillas.

>6 Roll up each tortilla and place seam side down in a baking dish.

>7 Pour the tomato paste over the burritos and sprinkle with the cheese. Bake in the preheated oven for 20 minutes.

>8 Remove from the oven and sprinkle with the scallions.

Transfer to a serving dish and serve
with mixed lettuce.

turkey schnitzel with potato wedges

serves 4

ingredients

4 russet potatoes
2 tablespoons olive oil, plus
    extra for shallow-frying

1 tablespoon dried sage
1 cup fresh white
    breadcrumbs

½ cup fresh finely grated
    Parmesan cheese
4 turkey cutlets

1 egg, beaten
salt and pepper
lemon wedges, to serve

>1 Preheat the oven to 425°F. Cut each potato into eight wedges.

>2 Place the potato wedges in a bowl, add the oil and 1 teaspoon of the sage, and season with salt and pepper. Toss well to coat evenly.

>3 Arrange the potatoes in a single layer on a roasting pan. Bake in the oven for about 25 minutes, until golden brown and tender.

>4 Meanwhile, add the breadcrumbs, cheese, and remaining sage to a bowl, season with salt and pepper, and mix together.

>5 Dip the turkey in the beaten egg and then in the crumb mixture, pressing to coat on both sides.

>6 Heat a shallow depth of oil in a skillet over high heat, add the turkey, and fry for 4–5 minutes, turning once, until golden brown. To check that the meat is cooked through, cut into the middle to check that there are no remaining traces of pink or red. Any juices that run out should be clear and piping hot with visible steam rising.

Serve the turkey hot with the potato wedges
and lemon.

shrimp noodle bowl

serves 4

ingredients

8 ounces rice noodles
2 tablespoons peanut oil
½ cup unsalted peanuts
1 bunch of scallions,
  diagonally sliced

2 celery stalks, trimmed and
  diagonally sliced
1 red bell pepper, seeded
  and thinly sliced
1 fresh Thai chile, sliced

1 lemongrass stalk, crushed
1¾ cups fish stock or
  chicken stock
1 cup coconut milk
2 teaspoons Thai fish sauce

12 ounces cooked, peeled
  jumbo shrimp
salt and pepper
3 tablespoons chopped
  fresh cilantro, to garnish

> **1** Put the noodles into a bowl, cover with boiling water, and let stand for 4 minutes, or prepare according to the package directions, until tender. Drain.

> **2** Heat a wok or deep, large skillet over medium–high heat, then add the oil. Add the peanuts and stir-fry for 1–2 minutes, until golden. Lift out with a slotted spoon.

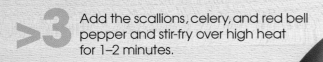

> **3** Add the scallions, celery, and red bell pepper and stir-fry over high heat for 1–2 minutes.

> **4** Add the chile, lemongrass, stock, coconut milk, and fish sauce and bring to a boil.

197

>5 Stir in the shrimp, then return to a boil, stirring.

>6 Season with salt and pepper, then add the noodles.

Serve in warm bowls, sprinkled with cilantro
and black pepper and the
toasted peanuts.

nut roast

serves 4

ingredients
2 tablespoons olive oil,
  plus extra for brushing
1 large onion, finely
  chopped
1 cup almond meal
  (ground almonds)
1 cup cashew nuts, finely
  chopped
1 cup fresh whole-wheat
  breadcrumbs
½ cup vegetable stock
finely grated rind and juice
  of 1 small lemon
1 tablespoon finely
  chopped rosemary leaves
salt and pepper
fresh rosemary sprigs and
  lemon slices, to garnish

>1 Preheat the oven to 400°F. Brush a rectangular 3-cup ovenproof dish with oil and line with parchment paper.

>2 Heat the oil in a large saucepan, add the onion, and sauté over medium heat, stirring, for 3–4 minutes, until soft.

Invert onto a serving platter and serve hot, garnished with rosemary sprigs, lemon slices, and extra black pepper.

>3 Stir in the almonds, cashew nuts, breadcrumbs, stock, lemon rind and juice, and rosemary. Season with salt and pepper and stir well to mix.

>4 Press the mixture into the prepared dish, brush with oil, and bake in the preheated oven for 30–35 minutes, until golden brown and firm.

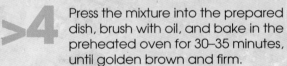

eggplant casserole

serves 2

ingredients

¼ cup olive oil
2 onions, finely chopped
2 garlic cloves, very finely
  chopped
2 eggplants, thickly sliced

3 tablespoons chopped
  fresh flat-leaf parsley, plus
  extra sprigs to garnish
½ teaspoon dried thyme

1 (14½-ounce) can diced
  tomatoes
1½ cups shredded
  mozzarella cheese

⅓ cup freshly grated
  Parmesan cheese
salt and pepper

> **>1** Heat the oil in a dutch oven or flameproof casserole dish over medium heat. Add the onions and cook for 5 minutes, or until soft.

> **>2** Add the garlic and cook for a few seconds, or until just beginning to brown. Using a slotted spoon, transfer the onion mixture to a plate.

> **>3** Add the eggplant slices to the pot in batches and cook until lightly browned. Transfer to another plate.

> **>4** Preheat the oven to 400°F. Arrange a layer of eggplant slices in the bottom of the dutch oven.

>5 Sprinkle with some of the parsley and thyme, and season with salt and pepper.

>6 Add layers of onion, tomatoes, and mozzarella cheese, sprinkling parsley, thyme, and salt and pepper over each layer.

>7 Continue layering, finishing with a layer of eggplant slices.

>8 Sprinkle with the Parmesan cheese and bake, uncovered, in the preheated oven for 20–30 minutes, or until the top is golden and the eggplants are tender.

Serve hot, garnished with parsley sprigs.

chili bean stew

serves 4–6

ingredients
2 tablespoons olive oil
1 onion, chopped
2–4 garlic cloves, chopped
2 fresh red chiles, seeded
  and sliced
1 cup drained and rinsed
  canned kidney beans
1 cup drained and rinsed
  canned cannellini beans
1 cup drained and rinsed
  canned chickpeas,
1 tablespoon tomato paste
3–3½ cups vegetable stock
1 red bell pepper, seeded and
  chopped
4 tomatoes, chopped
1 cup shelled fresh fava beans
1 tablespoon chopped fresh
  cilantro, plus extra to garnish
paprika, to garnish
sour cream, to serve

>**1** Heat the oil in a large, heavy saucepan with a tight-fitting lid. Add the onion, garlic, and chiles and cook, stirring frequently, for 5 minutes, until soft.

>**2** Add the kidney beans, cannellini beans, and chickpeas. Blend the tomato paste with a little of the stock and pour over the bean mixture, then add the remaining stock.

206

Garnish with the remaining chopped cilantro and a pinch of paprika and serve topped with spoonfuls of sour cream.

>3 Bring to a boil, then reduce the heat and simmer for 10–15 minutes. Add the red bell pepper, tomatoes, and fava beans.

>4 Simmer for an additional 15–20 minutes, or until all the vegetables are tender. Stir in most of the chopped cilantro.

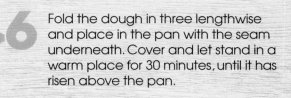

>5 Invert the dough onto a lightly floured surface and knead for 1 minute, until smooth. Shape into a loaf the length of the pan and three times the width.

>6 Fold the dough in three lengthwise and place in the pan with the seam underneath. Cover and let stand in a warm place for 30 minutes, until it has risen above the pan.

>7 Preheat the oven to 425°F. Brush the egg and water glaze over the loaf, then gently press the sunflower seeds all over the top.

>8 Bake in the preheated oven for 30 minutes, or until golden brown and hollow on the bottom when tapped.

Transfer to a wire rack to cool.

strawberry cheesecake

serves 8

ingredients

crust
4 tablespoons unsalted
  butter
1¾ cups crushed graham
  crackers
¾ cup chopped walnuts

filling
3 cups mascarpone cheese
2 eggs, beaten
3 tablespoons granulated
  sugar

9 ounces white chocolate,
  broken into pieces
2 cups hulled and
  quartered strawberries,

topping
¾ cup mascarpone cheese
2 ounces white chocolate
  shavings
4 strawberries, halved

> **1** Preheat the oven to 300°F. Melt the butter in a saucepan over low heat and stir in the crushed crackers and walnuts.

> **2** Spoon into a 9-inch springform cake pan and press evenly over the bottom with the back of a spoon. Set aside.

> **3** To make the filling, beat the mascarpone cheese in a bowl until smooth, then beat in the eggs and sugar.

> **4** Melt the white chocolate in a heatproof bowl set over a saucepan of gently simmering water, stirring until smooth. Remove from the heat and let cool slightly, then stir into the cheese mixture. Stir in the strawberries.

>5 Spoon the batter into the cake pan, spread evenly, and smooth the surface. Bake in the preheated oven for 1 hour, or until just firm.

>6 Turn off the oven and let the cheesecake cool inside the oven with the door slightly ajar until completely cold. Transfer to a serving plate.

Spread the mascarpone cheese on top,
decorate with the chocolate shavings, and
the strawberry halves and serve.

lemon meringue pie

serves 6–8

ingredients

pie dough

1¼ cups all-purpose flour,
plus extra for dusting
6 tablespoons butter, cut
into small pieces, plus extra
for greasing

¼ cup confectioners' sugar,
sifted
finely grated rind of
½ lemon
½ egg yolk, beaten
1½ tablespoons milk

filling

3 tablespoons cornstarch
1¼ cups water
juice and grated rind of
2 lemons

2 cups granulated sugar
2 eggs, separated

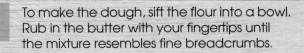

>1 To make the dough, sift the flour into a bowl. Rub in the butter with your fingertips until the mixture resembles fine breadcrumbs.

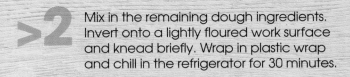

>2 Mix in the remaining dough ingredients. Invert onto a lightly floured work surface and knead briefly. Wrap in plastic wrap and chill in the refrigerator for 30 minutes.

>3 Preheat the oven to 350°F. Grease an 8-inch round tart pan. Roll out the dough to a thickness of ¼ inch, then use to line the pan.

>4 Prick all over with a fork, line with parchment paper, and fill with pie weights or dried beans. Bake in the preheated oven for 15 minutes.

>5 Remove the pie crust from the oven and take out the paper and weights. Reduce the oven temperature to 300°F.

>6 To make the filling, mix the cornstarch with a little of the water to form a paste. Put the remaining water in a saucepan. Stir in the lemon juice, lemon rind, and cornstarch paste.

>7 Bring to a boil, stirring. Cook for 2 minutes. Let cool slightly. Stir in ⅓ cup of the granulated sugar and the egg yolks. Pour into the pie crust.

>8 Beat the egg whites until stiff. Gradually beat in the remaining sugar and spread over the pie. Return to the oven and bake for an additional 40 minutes.

Remove from the oven, let
cool, and serve.

chocolate mousse

serves 4–6

ingredients

8 ounces semisweet dark
  chocolate, chopped
2 tablespoons brandy,
  Grand Marnier or
  Cointreau
¼ cup water
2 tablespoons unsalted
  butter, diced
3 extra-large eggs,
  separated
¼ teaspoon cream of tartar
¼ cup granulated sugar
½ cup heavy cream

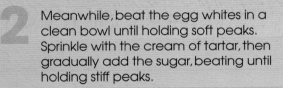

>1 Put the chocolate, brandy, and water in a heatproof bowl set over a small saucepan over low heat and stir until smooth. Remove from the heat. Beat in the butter and then the egg yolks, one at a time, until blended. Cool slightly.

>2 Meanwhile, beat the egg whites in a clean bowl until holding soft peaks. Sprinkle with the cream of tartar, then gradually add the sugar, beating until holding stiff peaks.

Spoon the mousse into bowls. Cover with plastic wrap and chill for at least 3 hours before serving.

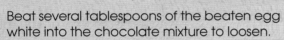 **>3** Beat several tablespoons of the beaten egg white into the chocolate mixture to loosen.

>4 Whip the cream until holding soft peaks. Spoon the cream over the chocolate mixture, then add the remaining egg whites mixture. Use a spatula to fold the chocolate into the cream and egg whites mixture.